Ballet

Kate Castle

Kingfisher Books

Kingfisher Books, Grisewood & Dempsey Ltd,
Elsley House, 24–30 Great Titchfield Street,
London W1P 7AD.

First published in 1989 by Kingfisher Books

BRITISH LIBRARY CATALOGUING IN PUBLICATION DATA
Castle, Kate
    Ballet and dancing.
    1. Dancing – For children
    I. Title   II. Series
    793.3
ISBN 0-86272-377-9

Edited by Deri Robins
Designed by Penny Mills
Cover designed by David Jefferis
Illustrated by Lynne Willey/*John Martin & Artists;*
    Amanda Appleby/*Maggie Mundy* and
    Peter Stephenson/*Jillian Burgess*

Phototypeset by Southern Positives and Negatives
(SPAN), Lingfield, Surrey
Printed in Spain

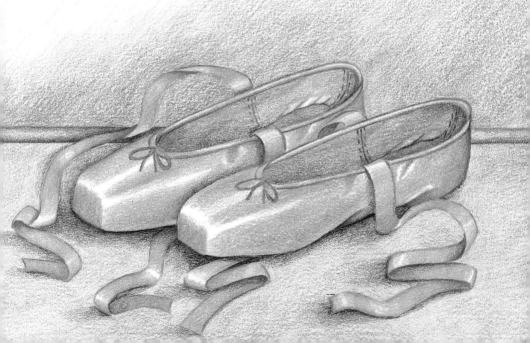

Contents

If you find an unusual or difficult word in this book, check for an explanation in the glossary on pages 30 and 31.

Curtain Up

In the theatre, the lights begin to dim. The audience falls silent as the orchestra strikes the opening notes, and the music swells. The curtain rises – and the ballet begins!

Ballet uses music, scenery, costumes and dance to tell a story. It makes its own magic, using the steps and movements to create a mood and weave spells. You may think it strange at first that no-one speaks. But if you watch carefully, you will begin to see that ballet has a special language all of its own.

The magic that you see on the stage is only part of the story. As you read this book, you will find out that every ballet is the result of a great deal of hard work by many different people.

Behind the Scenes

Here are some of the many people who work behind the scenes in a ballet theatre. Everyone here is busy rehearsing for the evening performance. Some people operate the lighting or change the scenery, while others adjust the costumes and make the 'props' which the dancers use on stage. And while all this is going on, someone has to clean the theatre, prepare the food for the company and sell tickets!

KEY
1. Stage manager
2. Lighting technicians
3. Scenery makers
4. Physiotherapist
5. Principal dancers
6. Scene shifters
7. Corps de ballet
8. Wardrobe mistress
9. Choreographer
10. Pianist
11. Conductor
12. Cleaners

A Dancer's Day

We can see how much hard work and preparation goes into a ballet by following Laura through her working day. She is a ballerina with a company which performs in a large theatre in a big city. Perhaps you know of a similar company near you? The company has a director to run it, and a choreographer who thinks up new ballets. Even though the dancers have trained for many years, they never stop learning or improving their skills.

The day always begins with class. Dressed in practice clothes, the dancers warm up by holding onto the barre.

8

A costume fitting. The wardrobe mistress is altering Laura's tutu.

Laura rehearses a pas-de-deux with her partner. They are practising new steps.

Laura carefully puts on her make-up, so that her features will show up under the bright glare of the lights.

The best part of the day! After the performance, Laura curtsies as the audience applauds her dancing.

Mime and Mood

Dancers learn the steps and movements of ballet rather as though they were learning to speak a language. The steps join together like sentences, and several sentences make a dance.

The ballerinas below are all dancing an arabesque. The first looks strong and confident. The second is much softer, while the third is so happy that she leaps right off the ground! You can see how the same step can suggest different moods or feelings.

BALLET TALK

Sometimes the dancers 'talk' in a special sign language called mime. Only ballets which are over a hundred years old use mime. There are more than two hundred different gestures altogether – the ones shown here are all from *Swan Lake*.

Plead   Death   Fear   King or Queen

Man   Love   Marry   Swear

3

How It All Began

Ballet began at the court of King Louis XIV of France, over three hundred years ago. At this time, ballets were slow and stately events. Over the years, teachers wrote down the steps and made them more lively and interesting. At first, only men danced in ballets. Then, when women were allowed to dance, they became more important on stage than the men. In modern ballets, both take an equal place on the stage.

Louis XIV dancing the role of 'The Sun King'.

These are some of the famous dancers who will never be forgotten.

Marie Taglioni

Anna Pavlova

Vaslav Nijinsky

In the clothes and boots they wore at King Louis' court, only slow, stiff steps were danced. Breakdancing would have been impossible!

Coppélia

Coppélia is one of the world's best-loved ballets. It tells the story of old Doctor Coppélius, who makes mechanical toys. His favourite is a doll called Coppélia, who looks so lifelike that a young man called Franz falls in love with her. He climbs into Doctor Coppélius' house, to meet the beautiful girl

Swanhilda dances with Franz and her friends, before they enter Doctor Coppélius' house.

he has seen smiling down at him from the balcony. In the meantime, Franz' girlfriend, Swanhilda, has crept into the house with some of her friends. They have great fun winding up all the toys. Swanhilda teases the old doctor cruelly by pretending to be Coppélia come to life, but he soon discovers that he has been tricked. Finally, Franz and Swanhilda marry, and celebrate with their friends. Old Doctor Coppélius is left all alone in his house of lifeless toys.

Going to Ballet School

If you are sure that you want to become a ballet dancer, you may be able to go to a special boarding school when you are eleven years old. As well as the daily ballet classes, the students have to learn ordinary subjects such as maths and geography. They also study music, folk dance, fencing and other sports. Male dancers have to become strong enough to lift their partners, as well as being as swift and skilful as a top footballer.

Boys develop their muscles by lifting weights. They have to build up strength but not bulk, which might slow them down.

As they get older, they will be strong enough to lift their female dancing partners with ease in a pas-de-deux.

Students often dance with professional ballet companies. They may appear in The Nutcracker, in the Christmas party scene – or as a soldier in the Rat King's army!

Starting to Dance

You don't have to go to a special boarding school to learn ballet. There are plenty of schools and dance centres which offer beginners' classes. Eight is a good age to begin dancing properly.

At the class a teacher will show you the steps and correct your mistakes, while somebody plays the piano or some taped music for you to dance to. You will need to wear special clothes at your ballet class, like the dancers in this picture.

In class, girls wear leotards and tights, while boys wear T-shirts, tights and socks. Soft ballet shoes help them to point their feet, jump quietly and spin easily.

BALLET SHOES

Boys' shoes are kept on with elastic, but girls have to learn to tie their ribbons. Cross them as shown here: first in front, then at the back, then at the front again. Tie them twice at the back, and tuck the ends in neatly. Loose ends are called 'pigs' ears'!

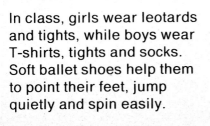

Starting to Dance – 2

Your first ballet classes will only be about half-an-hour long, so it is important to do lots of practice at home. Clear a space in your bedroom, and stand in front of a mirror. Use taped music if it helps.

Find out all you can about well-known dancers and companies. Perhaps you could persuade your teacher at school to take your class to see a ballet?

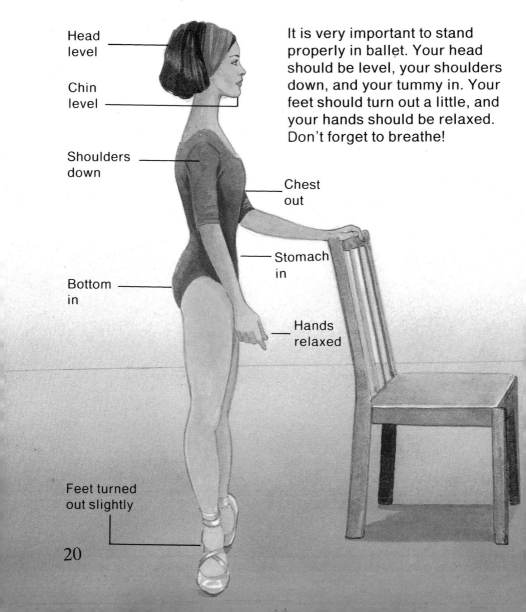

Head level

Chin level

Shoulders down

Chest out

Stomach in

Bottom in

Hands relaxed

Feet turned out slightly

It is very important to stand properly in ballet. Your head should be level, your shoulders down, and your tummy in. Your feet should turn out a little, and your hands should be relaxed. Don't forget to breathe!

THE FIVE POSITIONS

There are five positions of the head and arms in ballet. You can use them in many different ways, such as the first position of the feet and fourth position of the arms. When you begin, you will probably only use the first, second and third positions of the feet. The fourth and fifth positions are much harder, and you will learn these later. Every ballet step and movement begins and ends in one of these positions.

First Position | Second Position | Third Position | Fourth Position | Fifth Position

When you dance, always remember that you have something important to say to your audience. However hard the step may be, a good dancer will make it look easy! Grace and skill only come with lots of practice.

Steps and Movements

In class, the dancers begin with gentle exercises at the barre to warm up the muscles. They then move into the centre of the floor, to practise slow arm movements called port-de-bras, and adage, which uses arabesques and careful balances. Next come small neat jumps, called petits allegro, followed by large jumps across the studio called grands allegro. Some jumping steps use turns, or pirouettes.

These dancers are warming up at the beginning of a ballet class.

THE SEVEN MOVEMENTS

All the movements used in ballet are based on seven natural movements. These are bending, stretching, rising, sliding, turning, darting and jumping. Try each one yourself.

Plier means 'to bend'.

Glissade means 'to slide'.

A pirouette is a turning step.

This arabesque penchée uses a bending movement.

A pas-de-chat uses darting and jumping.

A Dance to Practise

Here is a ballet solo for you to try. Ready? Trois petits sautés, grand sauté, glissade, jeté en tournant, première arabesque, pirouette en dedans! Don't worry about the names, just follow the pictures and practise slowly, counting in your head. When you know the routine by heart, try dancing it in different ways, by changing the arm positions or adding more steps. You are becoming a choreographer! Try to find some suitable music to do your dance to.

1 Start in first position of arms and feet. Stand correctly, as shown on page 20.

2 Jump three times. As you do so, count 'and ONE and TWO and THREE . . .'

'And FOUR'! Make a huge jump, stretching out your arms and legs as far as you can.

Run quickly, then jump and turn in the air at the same time. Swing your arms up, too.

Slide your left foot up behind you, and stretch your right arm forward in an arabesque.

Quickly close your feet together. Spin twice on the right leg, and finish in any position.

Make Your Own Dance

Choreographers of new ballets often get their ideas from stories, poems, or pieces of music. You can make up your own ballet in the same way.

For example, think about the four seasons. What do they mean to you? Think about the weather, colours, celebrations and clothes, and try to put them into a dance. Spring might mean walking in the rain in wellingtons, with puddles and sudden sunshine!

Work out the steps with your
friends from ballet class.
Others may want to join in too,
as wardrobe mistresses or
make-up artists.

Putting on Your Dance

If you want to be really professional, you could make a model set to try out your ballet. The costumes and scenery will be easier to make if you have a clear drawing to work from first.

When you think your ballet is good enough to perform before an audience, design a poster and invite your friends. Write a programme, listing all those who have taken part. Perhaps you could ask friends who play instruments to join you?

Backdrop

Make slits

Make a model set from an old shoe box with one end cut out. Paint backcloths on separate pieces of card, and drop these in as and when you need them. Cut slits in the side of the box, as here, so that you can slide in your dancers.

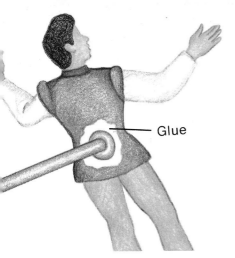

Glue

Draw your dancers onto card, paint them and cut out. Fix them onto knitting needles or lolly sticks, using glue or sticky tape.

A torch will give a good lighting effect. Try putting different-coloured paper or plastic over it. *Do not do this with any other light!*

The scenery should also be made out of card. It will stand up better if you bend back flaps at the side and base.

MAKE A POSTER

Your poster should be clear, colourful and eye-catching. It should tell your audience where and when the performance is taking place, and who is dancing. Look out for professional ballet posters, and decide which ones are the most eye-catching.

Glossary

Adage
Slow, stretching movements, such as arabesques, which help the dancers become strong and supple.

Arabesque
A position where one leg is lifted off the ground behind the dancer. There are five different arabesque positions.

Backcloth
A painted canvas cloth which is hung at the back of the stage as part of the scenery, or set.

Ballerina
One of the main female dancers.

Barre
The wooden hand-rail the dancers hold onto in class, during their warm-up exercises.

Choreographer
The person who thinks up new ideas for ballets, and works out all the steps for the dancers.

Conductor
The person who controls the orchestra. He waves a baton (small stick) to help the musicians keep time with the music.

Corps de ballet
The main group of dancers (rather like a chorus).

En pointe
Dancing on tiptoe, in shoes stiffened by hardened glue.

Glissade
A sliding step, where one foot follows after the other.

Grands allegro
Large jumping, travelling steps.

Jeté en tournant
When the dancer travels across the stage, then jumps and turns in the air at the same time.

Leotard
A costume worn by girls in ballet class with socks or tights. It looks rather like a swimsuit.

Mime
The sign language that dancers use.

Pas-de-chat
This means 'cat's step', and uses a darting and a jumping movement.

Pas-de-deux
A dance for two people.

Penchée
To 'tip up' – as in an arabesque penchée.

Petits allegro
Small jumping steps.

Physiotherapist
A person trained to treat dancers' injuries.

Pirouette
Really means 'spinning top'. In ballet it is the name for a turning step.

Plier
To bend the knees. Used in warm-up exercises, and in jumping movements.

Port-de-bras
The arm movements used in a ballet class, and in choreography.

Props
The objects that the dancers use on stage, such as dolls or swords.

Rehearsal
When the dancers and backstage crew practise the ballet.

Sauté
A jump. Trois petits sautés are three little jumps, and a grand sauté is a large leap.

Set
The scenery used in a ballet or a play.

Solo
A dance for one person only.

Stage manager
The person who is in control of everything during the performance of a ballet – including the lighting, scene changes, dancers and so on.

Tutu
A short frilly dress worn by ballerinas during a performance.

Warm-up
Simple exercises at the beginning of a class.

Index